The Winthrop Little

Book One
Operation Birthday Cake

Copyright registration number: TXU001806586
United States Library of Congress
Copyright Office

THE MEMOIRS OF WINTHROP LITTLE

No portion, characters, situations or themes of this book may be used, reproduced, scanned or distributed in any printed or electronic form without the written consent of Winthrop Little or his agent.

Copyright © 2012 Jeffrey A. Martin

All rights reserved.

ISBN: 0-692-92991-6
ISBN-13: 978-0-692-92991-9

Chapter One
Temptation Too Tall

Shay woke up early this morning, which is unusual for a Saturday. But it's his seventh birthday and he's so excited to get the day started. His mom and dad always make a big deal about birthdays and he is really hoping to get that yellow BMX bicycle he has wanted for so long. His mom and dad, Mr. and Mrs. Little, always let him sleep late on Saturdays. That's because he gets up early during the week for school and he's so busy with homework, basketball, guitar lessons, and his chores.

It's unfortunate for us that he woke up early today, because PJ and I didn't sleep a wink last night. And I, for one, could really use a few hours of sleep before Shay's big day. The reason we didn't get any sleep is a long story—and really all PJ's fault!

You see, PJ and I are Shay's teddy bears. PJ is a big brown bear. He's about ten inches tall. My name is Winthrop and I'm a gray short-haired bear—a full six inches tall! We sleep in Shay's gigantic double bed every night.

Most nights we are on the other side of the bed under the green tartan blanket Shay's grandmother brought from Ireland. But some nights he cuddles us in his arms while he sleeps. We love that! Hopefully he didn't try to cuddle us last night, though, because we snuck out of bed after he fell asleep, and we didn't return until just before he woke up. That was a really close call!

It would have been such a disaster if Shay woke up and we weren't there because he has no idea that we are alive. In fact, no humans know that we are, or that we have feelings and thoughts. Hopefully they know we have souls when they look into our eyes. It's hard to not blink when they do that, though!

Shay discovering our secret was not the only danger. Willie-B, who PJ and I suspect is a spy reporting to the KGB—the *Kommittee for Good Bears*—watches our every move. If he saw us do anything that goes against the *Pawbook for Good Bears*, he would report us. We suspect he had a paw in having Buttons removed from the house last year for what I thought was nothing. Of course, the Littles just thought Buttons got misplaced somewhere in the house and expect him to turn up some day.

WINTHROP LITTLE

Pawbook for Good Bears

DOs

- Always assume the last position in which a human saw you.

- Always have a blank expression and blank stare into space when people are around.

- Always love unconditionally.

- Always be cute and cuddly.

DON'Ts

- Don't ever leave your boy or girl alone in bed.

- Don't ever move things around the house.

- Don't ever eat the first piece of cake.

- Don't ever confuse your people or create any mysteries.

- Don't ever eat the last cookie.

Willie-B is only half an inch tall! He's a bright orange, hard plastic bear with no fur at all. He was a prize in a party cracker that Shay opened at Christmas dinner a few years ago. I think those crackers are an Irish tradition or something, with a toy and a paper crown inside. Shay's family is Irish. I mean, they are American now, but his grandparents came from Ireland. You see, everybody in America came from someplace else. Anyway, the Littles have all these Irish traditions. I like when people hold onto their heritage like that.

Shay's grandparents on his mother's side grew up in Derry, Ireland, which is on the River Foyle. His grandmother always talks about the old castles, the beautiful rolling green hills and says that nothing smells like the Derry air.

Last night's problems all started when PJ and I saw Mrs. Little bring in Shay's birthday cake yesterday afternoon. It was in a big blue and white box with a plastic window on top. And it was from the Bakery House. Everybody knows their cakes are the best!

Mrs. L put the box on top of the chest

freezer in the basement where it would be cool enough for the icing, but not too cold to make the icing go hard, which I hate. But if the icing is too soft, it gets all over our furry faces. I hate that, too! Oh, and of course, she wanted to keep the cake out of sight from Shay. As if he didn't know he was going to have a birthday cake!

Our big mistake, or should I say, PJ's big mistake, all started when Mrs. L left the house to go pick up Shay from school. We were all alone in the house. That's when we bears are allowed to have free reign of the home. It's great! With our superior sense of hear, we're always alert to when somebody is returning so we can resume our last-seen positions and blank stares.

Since we were all alone in the house, PJ wanted to go to the basement to check out the cake. Even then I knew it wasn't a good idea, but I figured there's no talking Peej out of it. We slid down the banister to the first floor. We do that a lot, and call it the *cubway*. As we were running through the foyer to get to the basement, I saw that several of Shay's shoes were scattered about the foyer, his baseball cap was on the newel post of the stair, and his sweatshirt was in a heap on the floor.

THE MEMOIRS OF WINTHROP LITTLE

We're not supposed to make noticeable changes to the human world. But, you see, Mr. and Mrs. L are sticklers about Shay picking up after himself. But he doesn't always do it. So if Willie-B can't see us, PJ and I sometimes clean up his messes to keep him from getting in trouble. It's all about protecting our boy, you know!

After we stacked the shoes in the closet,

hung the hat on a hook, and folded the sweatshirt to take upstairs with us, we took the basement cubway. We love that! You just have to watch out for the nail sticking out about halfway down. A bear could snag his fur and really do himself a mischief. When we got to the basement, the cake wasn't hard to find. We just had to follow our noses.

We climbed up onto the chest freezer using the cooling coils on the back of the freezer as a ladder. Those coils were hot, so I'm not sure why they are called cooling coils. Since they were hot, we scurried up. When we got to the top, we hoisted ourselves onto the box of rolls beside the cake box so that we could look in. We both gazed through the window of the box. But looking through the plastic window wasn't good enough for PJ. He wanted a closer look. So he used his claw to lift the tape off the lid of the box.

"Peej, I don't think this is a good idea."

"Oh Win, I just want to see it. Wow, it smells amazing! Smell the chocolate, smell the buttercream! Let's just take a look."

PJ lifted the lid of the box, and we both gazed in. We were mesmerized by what we saw inside.

Inside the box was a huge round cake as tall as PJ. It was covered with white buttercream icing and decorated with colorful plastic mummies and dinosaurs, and it had lots of colorful icing designs around the edges. Of course, "Happy Birthday Shay" was written on top in blue icing, since blue is Shay's favorite color. The high swirls of creamy icing and thick, decorative designs had a wet sheen like the icing was just put on the cake. The smell of the chocolate cake was so strong you'd think it was still baking in the oven.

The beauty of the fresh buttercream icing and the sweet chocolaty aroma was more than PJ could handle. I saw the look in PJ's eyes. He was fighting his desire and his lack of willpower.

I think I knew what was going to happen.

"No Peej!" But I was too late.

Without a moment's hesitation, he plunged his paw right into the top of the cake and took out a huge chunk! He stuffed that chunk of cake and mound of icing right into his mouth, getting icing all over his face.

"Oh man, Win, this is soooo good. You've got to have some!" He said with his mouth full of cake.

"PJ! Look what you did! That's Shay's cake! What are we going to do? If they find the cake like this, there's no telling what can happen! They might even blame Shay. And of course, he knows he didn't do this!"

PJ just sat there looking at me for a minute, blinking his eyes in his icing-covered face. "Gosh, Win, what have I done? I just couldn't help myself. You know how much I love cake."

"Let me think about this a minute. We can't let anybody find out about this, especially Willie-B. We don't want to end up with the same fate as Buttons!"

So, I sat there for a few minutes thinking about what we could possibly do to fix this damaged cake. I'm always the levelheaded one.

"OK, Peej, we're going to bake another cake, just like this one. We'll have to do it tonight after everybody has gone to bed. Then, after we've baked and iced the cake and copied all the decorations, we have to eat this entire cake to make sure it isn't found."

PJ just looked at me. I think he was becoming aware of the task we had ahead.

"I like the *last* part of the plan, Win!"

"How are you at piping icing?" I asked him.

"What's that?"

Chapter Two
Cubs Scout

We closed the lid of the bakery box. I looked at PJ. He was as much of a mess as the cake.

"Peej, we've got to get you cleaned up." I stood on my tippy toes and started licking the icing off his face. "Wow, that *is* good icing!"

After we got PJ all cleaned up, we headed upstairs. It's much harder going up the stairs and much less fun than taking the cubway down. Climbing stairs with steps that are taller than we are is no easy task. But we do it all the time, so we've gotten pretty good at it.

On our way upstairs to Shay's bedroom I wanted to detour into the kitchen pantry and climb the shelves to make sure there was a cake mix.

PJ and I had to do this climb together. We really have to do almost everything together, because when you live in a house built for humans, everything is so much bigger than we are. In fact, I can walk under the bed without even ducking! We have to work as a team, helping each other climb stairs and shelves, get onto a chair, a sofa, and of course, the bed, where we spend most of our time: "Pull me up"; "Push my tush!" "Put your foot in my paws, I'll give you a boost." We do that all day! We're strong bears, but we have to help each other because of the size of everything.

We got to the pantry, which is a small room between the foyer and the kitchen where a lot of food and kitchen stuff is kept. It took us a lot of effort to climb the shelves and resist the many temptations—an open bag of chocolate chips, a box of peanut butter cookies, a big jar of honey—which was especially tempting because we love honey. Well, we love chocolate too. Actually, we love most foods. Well, except for raisins and mushrooms. But chocolate and honey rank up there in our favorites. Now, if you combine chocolate and honey, wow, what a treat! And things with chocolate sprinkles . . . I can't even begin to tell you how much I love sprinkles! They're the perfect size for my mouth. But being really scared that we might not be able to pull off this enormous task, it was a bit easier to fight off the treats that were taunting us. We were focused and climbed the shelves with not even one nibble, and found the boxes of cake mix.

"Win, there's a yellow cake mix and a confetti cake mix. But there's no chocolate cake mix. Let's make the confetti. I love confetti! All those colorful specs in the white cake is so much fun!"

"No PJ, it has to be chocolate!" I said. Shay's mom bought a chocolate cake. If we made a confetti cake, she may have thought that the bakery made a mistake. But chocolate is Shay's absolute favorite. And I was going to make sure that our boy got his favorite cake for his birthday.

"You're right, Win. It wouldn't be the same for Shay if it's not chocolate. He loves chocolate as much as we do. But what are we going to do? There's no chocolate cake mix. I'd soooo hate to see him disappointed!"

"Oh, he *won't* be disappointed. We're going to bake him a chocolate cake from scratch." I didn't know anything about baking a cake, but there is nothing that PJ and I wouldn't do to make sure this is a great birthday for Shay. I'd even jump through rings of fire for him if I had to. I'm not sure why that would ever be necessary. I hope I never have to find out. But I'd do it all the same for him. And it makes me wonder—is my fur flammable?

Ok, now I'm curious, let me check my tag. It's hard to read, because it sticks out of my backside, so I have to really stretch and turn my head . . . "Not Flammable." PHEW!

"We better grab a cookbook and research

recipes."

Now, a cookbook, well almost every book, is twice as big as I am, and much heavier. Fortunately I was made with very strong stuffing, probably synthetic, so I can lift a lot of weight. I guess I'm like an ant. You know how you see ants carrying things that are much bigger than they are? Man, I hate being compared to an ant, though. Insects are gross!

Anyway, we jumped down and headed out of the pantry and across the kitchen to Mrs. L's office where the cookbooks are kept. The black-and-white checkered floor is very smooth and very slippery under our feet, so we were sliding around like we were on an ice skating rink. Normally it's lots of fun, but because we were in a hurry, it was a little frustrating.

Again, we used teamwork to climb the bookshelf to get to the cookbooks. We got to the third shelf and found the one I wanted, *Desserts, Desserts, and More Desserts*. Quite honestly, that is a book I've always wanted to look through. Can you imagine, a book all about desserts!? All these books about food! What a great concept! That seems more like something bears would come up with. But you have to paw it to people for coming up with books about food!

So there we were on the third shelf when we heard the garage door going up. We had to abort our mission. PJ and I jumped off the bookshelf and slid across the floor to get out of the kitchen before Shay and his mom came in. Normally we hear the car turning into the driveway because of our superior sense of hear. But we were so preoccupied with the mission, only the loud hum of the garage door jolted us back to reality.

We had to get back to the bedroom and resume our positions! We got into the foyer and were halfway up the stairs, pushing and pulling each other up each step, when we heard the back door open. I had grabbed the sweatshirt that we folded earlier, so I had that in tow as we were hurrying to get upstairs. This was not an easy task for little bears.

"Seamus Alan Little, come into the foyer. I want to show you something." We heard Mrs. L bellowing as she approached the foyer.

Mrs. L is a nice lady, and a very pretty lady, but she can be stern. I guess she's just trying to raise Shay to be a responsible person.

"How many times do I have to tell you to—that's odd. I could have sworn you left your things all over the foyer. I must be losing my mind. I'm sorry Pooh Bear." I love it when she calls him that!

"I guess I just have a lot on my mind."

It's always much better if we can get Shay's things cleaned up before his parents see the mess, but we can't always do that. I do have to admit, though, that PJ and I are amused by the little mysteries we seem to create.

We were hiding behind the newel post at the landing halfway up, where the stairs turn. Fortunately, Mrs. L returned to the kitchen without seeing us. I'm sure if she had seen us she would have yelled at Shay for leaving his bears on the stairs.

She went back into the kitchen and we continued up the stairs and into Shay's room. We climbed up onto the bed. It was very likely Shay would spend the rest of the afternoon doing his chores and playing with his friend, Thiago, from next door. Still, when our people are home it is always safer for us to stay on the bed.

Sitting on the bed for the rest of the afternoon gave me a chance to think about our predicament. If the Littles knew that we were really alive,

WINTHROP LITTLE

I could just go up to Shay's mom and tell her what we got ourselves into. I could say that PJ and I made a big mistake, and that we are very sorry. We could tell her it was too much temptation for a little bear, and that we would try to be better next time.

Now, I know of course, it's never easy to go up to somebody and admit you did something wrong. It takes a pretty big bear with a lot of courage to do that. But I know I'd feel pretty proud of myself if I did. And you thought it was easy to just be cute and cuddly. Now you can see it's not!

It seemed the only option left for PJ and me was to bake another cake, so we came up with our game plan while we sat on the bed. I must say, I was rather excited. Neither of us had ever cooked or baked anything, so this was going to be a new adventure for us. All we needed were little aprons and chef hats!

"Hey Peej, I have a great idea."

"What's that little buddy?" PJ got that from Shay. He calls us both that, all the time.

"If this cake thing goes well tonight, we could bake ourselves cakes all the time when the Littles aren't home."

"Win, you're a genius!"

Chapter Three
On a Mission

OK, so PJ and I were all psyched to bake the cake.

Everybody had gone to bed and nobody had gone down to the basement to look at Shay's birthday cake the rest of the day. We were so afraid that Shay's mom would want to show the cake to his dad. But nobody knew anything about what we—no, PJ—did to the cake.

Everybody was in bed, including us with Shay. But Shay was still wide-awake! I think he was excited about his birthday and hoping for that bike.

Next to eating, we love to be with Shay the most. But we were really eager to get going with the cake. I was starting to get fidgety, wishing Shay would fall asleep. But for the longest time, he was humming the song from his guitar lesson that he practiced all week (and we've heard about a million times). He was wearing his superhero pajamas and moving down under the covers like it was a fort or something. He was cuddling us and making voices for us, which sounded nothing like us. But, of course, he wouldn't know that.

After a while, Shay became still. He was

curled up on his side, with his back to us, and it seemed like his humming was fading. We waited a little longer. He became perfectly quiet. I thought he was asleep. Suddenly he flung around and was facing us, wide-awake, "Hey, where are my little buddies? There you are!"

As much as I love Shay cuddling me, we had to get going! Now that he was wide-awake, there was no telling how long it would be until he fell asleep.

PJ and I snuggled there in our boy's arms, listening to him hum a bit longer. Then the humming started to fade again. A few minutes later we noticed that his breathing was slow and regular like when he's asleep.

PJ and I looked at each other, wondering. We both looked up at Shay's face. He was drooling!

YES! He only drools when he's fast asleep!

PJ and I slowly slid ourselves out from under Shay's arm. We didn't want any sudden movement to wake him up. We learned long ago when we were sneaking a fistful of cookies while Mrs. L was home that sudden movements attract attention.

WINTHROP LITTLE

Finally, we were free. I looked up at our boy. I felt awful for leaving him there all alone. What if he needed us? If you can't count on your bears, whom can you count on? PJ knew what I was thinking. I'm sure he was thinking the same thing. But we had to bake a new cake.

The next obstacle was Willie-B. Was he asleep? The dresser where he sleeps is on the right side of the bed, right next to the door. If we shimmied down the covers on the left side of the bed, Shay would have blocked us from Willie-B's view. Although it was dark in there, bears have superior sense of see, just like our superior sense of sniff. So I was sure if we came down Willie-B's side of the bed he would have seen us, if he was awake. I wasn't exactly going to yell over to him to find out. PJ and I had to take our chances.

We climbed down, hanging onto the tartan blanket. If we jumped, Willie-B would hear the thud, soft though it would be. Like little mountain climbers, we repelled down the bed.

We made it to the floor. PJ put a claw to his mouth as if saying "shhhh." What did he think I was going to do? Scream, "We made it off the bed!" Really! I wasn't sewn yesterday.

At this point, I thought if we ever got out of the bedroom, baking the cake would be a breeze. I know now how wrong that was.

We slowly crept across the bedroom floor. We had to walk past the dresser where Willie-B stays to get to the door, which meant we had to pass right under Willie-B's nose. We paused. I didn't know if I could hear Willie-B breathing or if it was Shay. Anyway, we tiptoed our way to the door.

When Shay goes to bed, he shuts the door

because his mom and dad are still awake making noise downstairs. But when his mom and dad come upstairs to go to bed later, they come in to check on him, give him a kiss even though he's sound asleep, and leave his door wide open as they leave. I have no idea if they sleep with their bedroom door open or not. I've never gotten out of bed while Shay was asleep before.

So we slipped out into the hall. PJ pulled the door shut, almost completely closed, but not quite. This was a good idea because PJ and I would have to get back in and the smell of a baking cake wafting upstairs would be blocked by the closed door.

We looked down the hall and saw that the door to Mr. and Mrs. L's room was open. We had to shut that door, too. This was scary because we didn't know for sure if they were asleep yet. Their light was off, so there was a good chance they were asleep.

"Wait here, Win." PJ whispered. "I'll run down and pull the door shut." Since PJ is twice as big as I am, his legs are much longer. He can run much faster than I can. So I was glad that he ran down the hall to shut the door. It's sometimes hard to keep up with him when we do have the chance to run around the house.

PJ snuck down the hall, pulled the door shut, and was back to me in no time at all. With that, we jumped the cubway to the first floor. All the lights were off, but the house wasn't totally dark. Some light was coming in the windows from the moon and the streetlights in front of the house. We had no problem seeing where we were going.

We got into the kitchen. It was pretty dark in there, though. Doing our usual trick, we pulled out the drawers below the counter to use them as steps. We climbed up the drawers, hopped onto the counter, and were able to reach the light switch.

"Ah, light! That's better." PJ looked around. "Ok, Win. If you grab the cookbook, I'll . . . I'll . . . well geez. I don't know the first thing about baking a cake. So I don't know what I should do."

"Well, Peej, I need your help getting the cookbook down anyway. You can be the thumper." Long ago we learned that if we drop stuff, it would make a loud thud. So when we want to get things down to the floor to play with, we take turns being the thumper.

"Why do I have to be the thumper, Win? That book you were looking at earlier looks really heavy!"

"But you're so much bigger and a lot

stronger than I am." He isn't really stronger, but I thought it would help to butter him up.

"Let's do Rock-Paper-Scissors. Loser is the thumper."

I won with scissors. So PJ was the thumper after all.

"Hey Win, isn't there a recipe card instead of that huge book?"

"I'm sorry Peej, but I know we'll find a great recipe in that book."

This time, I climbed the shelf alone and got to *Desserts, Desserts, and More Desserts* while PJ sprawled out face down on the floor at the base of the bookshelf. I slid the book from its place on the shelf and over the edge so that it would land right on PJ.

THE MEMOIRS OF WINTHROP LITTLE

Success! The book did not make any noise, but PJ let out a big moan. That book had to hurt!

I jumped down and was able to start looking through the book. Oh my gosh, you should have seen the pictures of some of those cakes! You would have thought you were in heaven.

"PJ, I have to go down to the basement and have some of that cake right now. These pictures are making me so hungry!"

"Win, as hard as this is for me to say, we better not eat cake now. We have so much to do."

"Yeah, Peej, I guess you're right," I said, realizing that PJ really did understand the task ahead of us. "I'd better just pick a recipe."

Since I haven't ever baked, I wasn't sure what I was looking for. But I finally chose a recipe called *Grandma's Decadent Chocolate Cake*. How can you go wrong with that? Of course, we couldn't make it look like the picture. We had to make it look like the bakery cake that was downstairs. But it sounded really good.

I started to read the recipe.

"PJ, can you turn the oven on to 350?"

"Can you give me a boost up? I see a knob with numbers on it. 3...50...there we go. I think it's on."

"Pans. We need two large round pans." We started going through the cupboards until we found them.

I kept reading.

"PJ, it says to prepare the pans. Can you do that?"

"Sure." PJ said. He turned and looked at the pans. "Pans, you're about to go into the oven. Do your best, this cake is for Shay."

"No PJ!" I rolled my eyes. "I don't think it means to give the pans a pep talk. They're just inanimate objects."

"Winthrop, people think we're just inanimate objects, you know."

I don't think PJ is right about that. As I said earlier, I think that when people look into our eyes, they know that we have souls. I don't think the same can be said for cake pans. They don't even *have* eyes!

"Peej, haven't you ever snuck around the kitchen when Shay's mom is baking? I think I've seen her spread butter and flour around the pan. I'm going to assume that that's what 'prepare the pans' means."

Man, you have to know a lot to bake. I wonder if it gets easier the more you do it. Fixing Shay's old bike got easier every time we did it. The chain kept coming off. When Shay wasn't around, PJ and I would put it back on. The first time we did it, we got really dirty and had to sneak into the washing machine with the laundry. Fortunately, Mrs. L was washing towels and not underwear.

But anyway, the more we fixed the old bike, we learned what we were doing. I bet baking is the same.

PJ started to get the pans prepared. So I thought I'd start getting the cake batter going. I read through the recipe to see what we would need. The first ingredient listed was four eggs.

"Hey Peej, I'm going into the refrigerator to get some things. Can you come hold the door open? I'll paw you some things, too."

So I climbed the shelves of the refrigerator and found the eggs in a carton on a shelf toward the top of the door. There were five eggs. Great!

"PJ, I'll drop you the eggs, one at a time. Can you catch them, then put them in the glass bowl?"

"Ready, Win."

"OK, here comes." I dropped the first egg.

SPLAT! It hit the floor and cracked open.

"PJ!"

"I know, I know. Drop another one. I'll catch this one, I'm sure."

"You better! We only have four eggs left, and we need all four." I was really nervous now. We didn't have an egg to spare! If PJ missed another egg, our cake would not turn out. Of course, I didn't consider until now that the eggs might be missed at some point. I'll have to worry about that later.

"OK, here comes another egg . . ."

PJ caught it!

"Wait while I put the egg in the bowl. I'll be right back."

I dropped two more eggs that PJ caught

successfully, and very carefully placed into the bowl. He stepped in the broken egg a few times and was tracking raw egg around the room. It's slimy and gross. I was thinking I'd have to watch out where I walk when I get down there.

"OK, Peej, this is our last egg. You've gotta catch it."

I slowly let it slide out of my paws. I watched as it hurled down to PJ. He was looking up at me. All I could see was the checkered floor, PJ looking up, and the egg falling, almost in slow motion . . . he caught it!

At this point, I thought the hard part was over. But no! Figuring out what the recipe was calling for was very difficult. I had no idea what a *tsp* or *tbsp* or *1/2c* meant. Actually, I hadn't seen words without vowels before. I used my best guess. We had to go back and forth between the pantry and the kitchen several times hauling all the ingredients. This involved a lot of shelf-climbing for me, and poor PJ was the thumper every time. No wonder he had sore stuffing for days after that.

Finally, we got to the part of the recipe that called for cocoa powder. I located it on the shelf and pushed it over. As soon as it landed on PJ he could tell by the smell what it was. "Win, this is chocolate. We deserve a little break and snack. Let's have some of this chocolate powder. It will be like a chocolate Pixy Stick."

We each reached a paw into the tin and took a huge pawful of cocoa and put it in our mouths. Yuck! It was so bitter. We were both spitting it out. It was awful.

"I think we better put extra sugar in the cake. I doubt if the cookbook knows that our cocoa powder is so bitter." I said to PJ.

"Good idea, Win. We better put twice as much sugar in as it says."

"Oh, at least!" I said.

We were almost done getting all the ingredients into the big glass bowl. The flour was the last ingredient to add. I dumped it in on top of everything else.

"Now, PJ, we need to mix it all up. We better mix it a lot, to make sure the eggs get cracked, and the shells broken up completely. Guess we should use the electric beaters."

We found the paw-held mixer, which humans call "hand-held," in the bottom drawer, and we found the beaters with the utensils. PJ, being much bigger, decided to hold the mixer, and raising my paws over my head, I held the bowl steady.

"OK, Win, here goes!" With that, PJ

turned the mixer on. The switch slid all the way to high. Flour went flying everywhere! PJ and I were both covered in white powder. PJ looked like a ghost!

"Stop the mixer, stop! Stop!"

PJ turned off the mixer. But we were both covered with flour and it was all over the floor and cabinets, too.

I looked around. The kitchen was a disaster! There were open containers everywhere. The cocoa tin, the bag of flour, the bag of sugar, and the bottle of vanilla extract were all turned over. A bottle of oil was dripping on the floor. We never put the lid back on it. And of course there was raw egg all over the floor. It was a MESS!

"Uh oh, Peej, we have a lot of cleaning to do."

"Let's get this cake made first, then we'll tackle that, little buddy." PJ was still determined to get this cake made. That made me feel better.

"OK, I'll get some more flour to replace what went flying. Why don't you keep mixing to get the eggs all broken up." I dragged the bag of flour over to the mixing bowl. That bag was way bigger than I am, but I was able to drag it over.

I grabbed a soup spoon and used it like a

shovel to slowly add flour as PJ was mixing the batter with the electric mixer. I had no idea how much to add.

"I'll tell you when to stop, Win. But for now, keep shoveling."

I did. It seems like I put almost the entire bag in. Finally I peeked over the side of the bowl. It was taller than I am, I had to get on my tippy toes, reach the rim of the bowl and hoist myself up. I was leaning over the side of the bowl, looking in. Something didn't look right to me.

"PJ, it looks awfully light and very dry. I don't think it will be chocolaty enough. I have an idea. I saw a bottle of chocolate syrup in the refrigerator. I'll grab that and we can squeeze some into it."

"I have an idea too, Win. Cake and ice cream go great together. I'm going to grab some chocolate ice cream out of the freezer, we can put some right into the cake!"

"Great idea!" Bears love ice cream. We also put a few toothpicks into the batter. I've heard the cooks on TV talk about putting a toothpick into the cake for some reason. So if you're supposed to put one in, a few more would make it even better. So we put a few in to make sure it would be great.

Well, we finally got the cake batter just

perfect. We were really happy with the way it looked. Like all good cooks, we had to have a taste. Yup, PJ and I stuck our paws into the bowl, and it tasted great! I got a little eggshell in my mouth, but what would you expect with cake batter?

We divided the batter into the cake pans. Getting them into the oven was no easy task, let me tell you. Just opening the oven door was very difficult.

We came up with a plan. We found a ball of string in the junk drawer where the scissors and pens and keys (that nobody knows what opens) are all stashed. We threw the string up, trying to get it over the oven door handle and back down. It missed! It took eight tries before the ball of string went between the oven and the handle and back down the other side, but we finally got it and were able to pull the door open.

It took both of us to hoist the cake pans filled with batter up onto the oven door. Then I hoisted PJ up.

"Ouch, ouch! The oven door is hot!" PJ jumped down to the floor.

"Here, PJ." I pawed him an oven mitt. Put this on the oven door to stand on." So we hoisted the oven mitt up to the oven door too.

I helped PJ once again get onto the oven door. Then I pawed him the really long spatula that Shay's dad uses on the outside grill. It was hanging in the pantry next to the apron that says, "Kiss the Cook." PJ used the long spatula to lift the cakes onto the baking rack in the oven.

After he got the cakes into the oven, PJ jumped down and we pushed the oven door shut with a bang.

"OK, Win, while the cakes bake, we have a lot of cleaning up to do. Then while they're cooling, we can make the icing."

"Shhh! PJ, did you hear that?" I heard a noise upstairs. "Somebody is coming down here."

"Quick, turn out the lights!" PJ climbed the open drawers to get onto the counter to turn off the lights.

We stood perfectly still. We heard Shay's dad walking in the upstairs hall toward the top of the stairs. "I think I heard something downstairs. I'm going to go down and check it out." Mr. L was headed toward the stairs.

We heard Mrs. L's voice in the bedroom.

It was very quiet for a moment. Then we heard Mr. L speak.

"I peeked in on Shay, He's sound asleep. Strange, though, I could have sworn I left his door wide open when I checked in on him earlier, and now it was closed."

After another moment of silence, we heard his footsteps as he slowly came down the stairs, pausing on each step, listening for sounds coming from downstairs. Finally we could see that he was at the bottom of the stairs. The foyer was brighter than the kitchen, with the moonlight and streetlight streaming in the front windows. We could see his silhouette as he slowly worked his way through the foyer toward the kitchen.

He stopped in the doorway of the kitchen. PJ and I were frozen stiff with fear as he came into the doorway. I knew his hand would brush up against PJ as he reached for the switch. I knew PJ had not moved from there. What would we do when the lights came on and Shay's dad saw the kitchen messier than it had ever been, with egg all over the floor, flour and cocoa powder strewn about, bags of flour and sugar and bottles overturned everywhere, and PJ and me standing there in the middle of it all?

Uh oh!

THE MEMOIRS OF WINTHROP LITTLE

Chapter Four
Mission Melt Down

Shay's dad stood in the doorway of the kitchen, in the dark, for only a few seconds. But we were in such suspense for what was about to happen that it seemed like he was there for six years with his hand on the light switch. It was so quiet, you could hear a pin drop.

Well, a pin didn't really drop, but if one did, you could hear it.

But what made him stop in his tracks had to be a miracle. As he reached for the light switch, the wind blew a tree branch and it brushed against the side of the house. He turned in the direction of the noise. Then we heard it again.

With that, Mr. L turned in the dark and went back into the foyer, and headed back upstairs. "I've got to get those branches trimmed. Everything seems fine down here."

Yeah, right! Everything's fine? I don't think so. If he had seen that mess! I get nauseous when I think about it! And that's saying something. Have you ever seen your bears get nauseous? Not very often, I bet.

"Oh my gosh, Winthrop! That was a close call!" I could hear the relief in PJ's voice. We waited there a little longer in the dark, perfectly still, until we were sure that Mr. L was back in his room, and hopefully back in bed, before PJ turned the lights back on.

While the cake was baking, we got the kitchen cleaned up. We had to lug all the bags of flour and sugar back into the pantry, as well as the oils, baking powder, cocoa powder, and so many other things. We got them all put back into the exact same spot where we found them. It was much harder to get them back up onto the shelves than to push them off the shelf onto PJ. It took teamwork, but we did it. Then we got out the cleaning sponges to clean all the mess that was somehow all over the kitchen. With our claws we cut slits into the tops of the sponges and stuck our feet in. That way we could skate around, cleaning with sponge skates on our feet.

I hate cleaning up after cooking. Mixing the cake batter was a lot of fun. But I can't say the same for cleaning up the mess. Why does cooking have to be so messy? Perhaps it has something to do with the fact that we're actually much smaller than most of the packages of ingredients and the utensils.

Wiping the flour and cocoa was more difficult than I thought it would be. It seemed like we were just smearing it around. We kept wiping and wiping. After a lot of skating, it was starting to look cleaner. PJ got a little bit carried away skating in figure eights with his arms stretched out.

"Win, look at me! I'm an Olympic finger skater." Then he threw his paws over his head and spun around in a pirouette.

"PJ, it's *figure* skater. Now quit playing around. You aren't even cleaning, you're skating *around* the egg!"

EDITOR'S NOTE: *Although Winthrop Scolded PJ For Getting Carried Away With His Skating, This Picture Is Evidence That Winthrop Was Playing, Too.*

The egg! If anything is impossible to do, it's gotta be cleaning dried raw egg! Just skating with our sponges was not good enough. We had to use our claws to scrape it off the floor.

While we were cleaning, we kept looking at the clock. The recipe said to bake the cake for 60 minutes. We could smell the cake as it baked and it smelled amazing! The closer it got to the 60-minute mark, the more chocolaty it smelled.

We finished cleaning just as it was time to take the cake out of the oven. Wow, it took a whole hour to clean up our mess! We pulled on the string to open the oven door, PJ tossed the oven mitt up onto it, and I hoisted him up again. I pawed him the long-handled spatula, then I crawled up the drawers to reach the oven dial and turned it off.

PJ used the long spatula to take the pans out of the oven. Come to think of it, that long spatula was like a wooden peel that Italian chefs use to take a pizza out of a pizza oven. I love pizza. Mushrooms are about the only food I don't like, so I don't like pizza with mushrooms on it. Oh, and raisins. I don't like raisins either. But I've never heard of putting raisins on pizza, anyway.

"Win, the cake looks perfect! I can't wait for a taste!"

"NO! PJ, we are not eating this cake! Keep saying Shay, Shay, Shay. Then you'll have the willpower to keep your paws out of the cake."

"I know, I know." PJ sounded disappointed. "I guess we should let them cool."

"Yeah, while they cool, we'll make the icing. Buttercream. Yum!"

I found a recipe for the icing. I wish I had thought to look for it when we started the cake. It called for lots of room-temperature butter. All the butter we had was in the refrigerator and hard as a rock. And we didn't have enough of it.

"Peej, the butter that we do have is way too hard. Let's put it next to the warm cake, that way it will get soft faster."

"I'll get the butter, Win. You keep reading the recipe and figure out what else we need."

I looked around the kitchen, examining different ingredients. I had to figure out what to use since we didn't have enough butter. I found a can of shortening in the pantry. It looked like it was the same consistency of soft butter, so I grabbed that. It didn't look like there would be enough of that either, so I kept looking. Bingo, I found just what would do the trick; a full jar of mayonnaise.

So we put the butter, shortening, and mayonnaise in a large, glass mixing bowl. We couldn't find any confectioner's sugar, so we dumped an entire box of cornstarch in. Cornstarch looks the same as confectioner's sugar, so I was sure it would be fine. I remember what confectioner's sugar looks like. Mrs. L sprinkles it on chocolate crinkle cookies, one of my favorites!

PJ climbed up to mix it with the electric mixer.

"Stop!" I whispered, but very loudly. I had to make sure PJ didn't turn on the mixer. "Remember what happened last time? We're still wearing the flour. Turn it on low and slowly work the beaters into the mixture, Peej."

"Oh, right, right. Thanks for reminding me Little Buddy."

We got the icing all mixed up. It looked pretty good. I tasted it. It wasn't as good as the bakery icing, but humans don't have quite as refined a sense of taste as we bears do. They wouldn't notice the difference.

"Win, we need different colors of icing for the decorations. How do we do that?" PJ was right. We had to decorate the cake to look the same as the cake that *he* ruined, so we would need different colors of icing, for sure.

"I've got it! In the craft cupboard by the kitchen table is a whole bucket of Shay's tubes of paints. We'll just separate the icing into a few bowls, and squeeze some paint into each bowl of icing, mix it around, and that should give us different colors of icing." I'm so smart!

"Gee, Win, I don't know." PJ said. "I don't think you can eat paint."

"PJ, would they keep it here in the kitchen if it couldn't be eaten?"

"Hmmm. I guess you're right."

Wow, I've never baked before, and here I was, figuring out what people go to cooking school for years to do! I'm pretty proud of myself.

"Win, I think we need to go downstairs and take a look at the cake again, if we're going to copy it exactly. And while we're examining it, why don't we have some? I'm hungry!"

"Peej, that's a great idea." I was getting really hungry, too, from all the baking and cleaning. "And, you know, we do have to eat it all up, anyway. We might as well start now!"

So we headed downstairs. Sliding down the cubway, we got there in no time at all. We lifted the lid, and before we even examined the cake, we both dug our paws in and took a chunk out.

"Wow, Peej, this is great cake!"

"Tell me about it!"

We sat there awhile, stuffing our faces with cake. We almost forgot to examine the decorations so that we could copy it. But suddenly I remembered our mission, and before we ate too much, we looked it over and locked that cake into our photographic memories.

"Win, do you think we can make our cake as pretty as this one?" PJ asked. I think he was concerned that, because this was our very first effort *ever* at baking and decorating a cake, we couldn't make it as good as the bakery.

"Sure, there's nothing to it. I mean, how hard can it be to spread icing?" I was super confident now that I had just baked my first cake, and it turned out great!

We returned upstairs to the kitchen and got busy assembling our cake and covering it with icing. Icing a cake that was taller than I am was not as easy as I expected it to be.

I found the piping bags in a drawer. It was so hard to use those things. After the difficult task of getting the icing into the bags, I squeezed the bag to get the icing all the way down to the tip so that I could start edging the cake. But since these bags were bigger than me, squeezing them meant giving them a bear hug, which we bears just call a hug.

I guess I squeezed too hard, because a stream of icing shot out and hit PJ right in his face. I laughed so hard because a string of icing was dangling from his nose and it was swinging when he turned his head to scold me. PJ was none too pleased, to say the least.

I finally calmed down and was able to carry on icing the cake. This was my first time making fancy icing decorations and manipulating the bag to make the swirls took more practice than I had time for. So I just made icing blobs around the cake. Squeezing the bag to get the icing out took a lot of my strength, so PJ did the writing.

'H-a-p-p-y B-i-r-f-d-a-y S-h-'

"Win, I ran out of room on the cake."

"I guess we'll just have to put the rest of

his name below."

'a-y!'

"We're done!" PJ was so pleased to have the cake all made. "Stand back and look at it. It's absolutely perfect!"

I wasn't so sure. After all, I am a perfectionist.

The cake looked *almost* perfect.

There was one very slight flaw that bothered me. The color of the icing we made for the writing was a very slight shade lighter blue than what the bakery used.

But that's a detail that only I would pick up. Other than that, it *was* perfect!

After PJ and I stood there admiring our work for a few minutes, I realized we were not done yet.

"Now, Peej, all we have to do is to switch out the cakes." I had not thought about how we were going to get our cake down to the basement and up into the cake box on the freezer.

"Well, Win, we can't exactly slide the cake down the cubway."

"No, but we've got to figure something out."

I could see that PJ was thinking.

"Cubway . . . hmmm. Win, I have an idea. We can make the cake it's own cubway! Or should I say cakeway?"

"What are you talking about, Peej?"

"That enormous cardboard box from the new refrigerator is still downstairs. We can cut a strip of cardboard and put it on the stairs like a ramp. We'll put the cake on Shay's skateboard. We can use the ball of string from the oven door to lower the cake down the stairs."

I have to paw it to PJ. Usually I am the genius, but this time he came up with a brilliant idea. I'm sure I would have come up with that idea, but I think I had used up all my ideas getting the cake made.

So that was the plan.

But guess where Shay's skateboard was. Yeah, in his bedroom. We had to go back upstairs to where he was sleeping and get that blasted skateboard out.

After all the effort to get upstairs, we started the next task of getting the skateboard out of the room, undetected. We were exhausted by this point, too, so it was even more difficult.

Earlier in the day, the skateboard was on the floor by the bed. But before Shay went to bed, he cleaned up his room and put it in the closet.

The closet has sliding doors, which are pretty easy to open. You just have to put your paw in and slide the door over, which PJ did. The skateboard was right there, on the floor, nothing on top of it. Excellent! For once, something was going to be easy. It has wheels, so all we had to do was push it out of the closet and out of the room.

I got behind the skateboard and gave it a little push.

Squeak! The wheel bearings needed to be oiled. There was no time for that, but I put it on my list of things to do in the future.

That squeak made us stop dead in our tracks. Did we wake up Shay?

No, but I heard Willie-B stir and get up. It's hard for him to be quiet. We heard his hard plastic footsteps as he walked across the dresser. Although it was dark in the room, we could see him as he stood on the edge looking in our direction. PJ and I ducked back into the closet. He seemed to be at the edge of the dresser for like six years! So we waited.

Finally, we heard him return to his bed, an old velvet ring box that Shay commandeered from his mom. We waited a bit longer to make sure he was asleep. Then PJ lifted one end of the skateboard and I lifted the other end. We carried it out of the room and down the hall. We couldn't take the cubway to get downstairs with a skateboard, so I jumped down to the next lower step and PJ slid the skateboard down, then he jumped down. We did that until we got to the bottom of the stairs.

We made it to the kitchen. PJ and I lifted the cake onto the skateboard, tied the string onto it, and got it to the top of our cardboard ramp. We slowly lowered the

skateboard down the ramp. The cardboard sagged a lot under the weight of the cake, and

THE MEMOIRS OF WINTHROP LITTLE

a few times I thought it would collapse. But we got the cake all the way down to the basement floor without a disaster.

PJ and I slid down the cardboard ramp, so there was no fear of a nail snagging our bums this time!

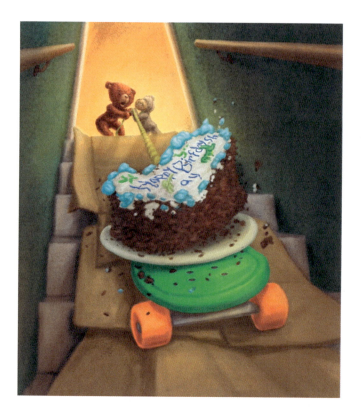

Next, we had to get our cake up onto the freezer and switch it with the partially eaten one in the bakery box. But our cake was at the bottom of our makeshift ramp on the basement floor. By throwing the ball of string up and over some pipes in the basement ceiling and looping it around both ends of the skate board, we were able to rig up an elevator to lift our cake up.

It wasn't as easy as it sounds. It took several tosses to get the ball of string up and over those pipes. We had to loop it over a few times to create a pulley elevator system. But we finally got it to work. PJ and I stood on the floor, and we both pulled on the string that looped up to the ceiling pipes and back down to the skateboard. As we pulled on the string, the skateboard rose up with the cake on it. We finally got our cake up there.

We opened the box and slid the bakery cake out onto the top of the freezer. We took our cake off the skateboard, put it in the box, and closed the lid.

Now all we had to do was to get rid of the bakery cake.

"Guess we have to eat this, huh, Win." PJ would usually be much more eager to eat a chocolate cake than that. But he was really tired. We were both really tired. Bears need a lot of sleep you know. In fact, some bears sleep all winter!

So we ate, and we ate, and we ate.

THE MEMOIRS OF WINTHROP LITTLE

We got about halfway through the cake. Which is a lot of cake for two little bears. Our bellies were really full. I mean, *really* full. And mine was starting to hurt and I was concerned that I might burst a seam.

"PJ, I can't eat any more."

"Me neither, but what are we going to do with all this cake?"

"I've got an idea." Now my brilliance was kicking back in. "Let's hide it behind the washing machine over there. Then we can come back later and eat the rest of it."

So that's what we did. We used our skateboard elevator to lower the rest of the cake to the floor, then we dragged it across the basement and put it behind the washing machine. We planned to come back another day to finish eating it.

After we dismantled the cardboard ramp, our task was done.

What a night. As we headed upstairs with the skateboard in tow, we noticed it was getting lighter outside. The sun was coming up. It was later than we thought. Operation Birthday Cake took all night.

We crawled into bed and got under the covers. We were expecting Shay to sleep late like he usually does on Saturday, and we were really looking forward to being cuddled up in Shay's arms for the next few hours, fast asleep.

But that wasn't to be. Just as we pulled the covers up to our noses, Shay rolled over and looked at us.

"Are my little buddies ready to get up? It's my birthday today!

Chapter Five
Smashing Sucess

That was another close call, and you can see why PJ and I didn't get a wink of sleep. We could nap during the day, but we do a lot of that sort of thing. Since today is the day of Shay's big birthday party, we weren't about to nap on the bed and miss seeing any of it.

I bet people probably envy us bears, sitting around and napping all day. Well actually, it gets pretty boring. And besides, our bums get sore if we just sit there all the time. So we do stuff that sometimes causes a little bit of mischief.

We move stuff around, which makes our family think they're going crazy. Shay's mom will put down a pen or something and we'll grab it when she turns away. Then, when she turns back and it's gone, she goes bonkers looking for it, saying stuff like, "I know I just put it down right here!" We'll eat the last piece of some leftover food, usually a cookie. Or cake. Or pie. Man, PJ loves pie! Or we'll drink all but the last little bit of milk or juice and put the container back. One of my favorites is to take one sock out of the laundry basket, then return it a few weeks later.

It was during one of the times that PJ and

I were bored and we were sneaking around the kitchen when we heard Shay's mom on the phone planning his party.

All of Shay's friends would be coming over to play some games, then they're going to have a cookout with burgers and hot dogs, and then our cake! I can hardly wait! PJ and I love parties!

But get this. Mrs. L told the other moms *not* to bring any presents. She said they were trying to stress that the importance of celebrating was being with people you care about, and not the presents. She said their kids could *make* a card if they wanted to, and that she was hoping each mom would put a check into a sealed envelope for the amount they would have spent on a present for Shay. The sealed envelopes would ensure that nobody would know the amount of the check. So it could be for as much or as little as they wanted. Nobody would ever know. After the party, probably on Monday, Shay and his mom would take the envelopes to a charity that Shay selected and make the donation in Shay's name for his birthday. Mrs. L told the moms that she wanted Shay to learn that there are always others who are much less fortunate. She wanted to teach Shay that we must all do what we can to help others, even if it means some self-sacrifice. And giving up presents is minor in the big picture.

At first, I didn't like this idea at all because I love presents. I mean, who doesn't! Presents? Come on! So she didn't think that not getting presents was much of a sacrifice. Geez! I thought it was.

But then PJ reminded me that Shay would be getting plenty of presents from his mom and dad, his aunt and uncle and grandparents, and of course his best friend Thiago. Then, when Shay chose the local animal rescue as his charity, because he wanted to make sure that all the dogs and cats got good care, I really liked this idea. Animals can be kind of scary to a little bear like me, but they need help too. And they're such great companions to people. They always love unconditionally, much like us bears, actually, and almost as cuddly.

Shay was really excited about making a difference, so I was really proud of him!

And you know what? The more I thought about it, I realized how great I'd feel knowing that I, Me, Winthrop Little, was going to be helping someone in need and that I, too, would be making a difference in the world. I think that's kind of cool!

I like the Idea of this party so much that I call it a "Shay Party". You could try it too for your next birthday. Check out the charities near you that could benefit from donations and let your friends know."

Shay cuddled us for just a few minutes, then he got up, made his bed, placed us in the middle against the pillows—our usual spot—then put on the old clothes he wears when he helps his dad with outside chores. He and his dad spent the better part of the morning setting up for the party. Shay swept the patio with a broom and wiped off the patio furniture while his dad ran streamers and hung balloons. Then they set up folding tables and chairs. Shay's mom was in the kitchen getting the food ready. PJ and I peeked out the bedroom windows, watching Shay and his dad. It looked like it was going to be a beautiful day, not too hot. Just right! I wish we could have been down there helping.

Finally, Shay came upstairs to start getting himself ready. His mom told him he had to take a bath. She even told him to wash behind his ears. What did she think was back there, anyway?

While our boy was getting ready and PJ and I were sitting on the bed, Shay's dad was helping his mom get the food ready to take out to the patio.

"Marty," that's Shay's dad, by the way. His real name is Martin, but everybody just calls him Marty. "Would you go downstairs and bring up the cake? It's on top of the freezer." We heard his mom say.

"Since it's not too hot out, I think it would be nice to have the cake on display."

We knew Shay would be a while in the bathtub. He loves his baths. He likes to play with his mechanical submarine and a plastic shark. As far as I know, the shark isn't alive like we are. Boy, can you imagine being in the tub with a live shark? Yikes!

Since PJ and I knew we had some time, we snuck downstairs. We wanted to see Mr. L bring our cake up out of the basement and take it out of the box. We knew he would rave at how beautiful the cake looked. Although, he'd think it was the bakery cake, of course.

We got downstairs just as he was coming up with the cake. We peeked into the kitchen from the dining room door—it was a safe place to hide where we were still able to see.

And since the party was outside on the patio, nobody would be coming through that door.

Just as Shay's dad got to the top of the stairs, his right foot slid out from under him and he lost his balance. He threw one hand in the air to steady himself. The cake box teetered in his other hand.

"Oh, oh!" Shay's dad was shouting.

Then the box tipped out of his hand, the lid came open, and the cake tumbled out and fell to the floor.

Shay's mom was screaming, "Martin, what are you doing?! Be careful!"

But it was too late. Our beautiful cake was in a heap on the floor. It was just one massive blob.

Mr. L just stood there in shock, silent for several moments, looking at the cake on the floor. It was totally destroyed! PJ and I were in shock too. I mean, our beautiful cake on the floor! I could feel my fur stick straight out!

"Oh my gosh PJ, all that work we did—for nothing!" I said.

"And all that lost sleep and lost cuddle time with Shay . . . but Win, I have to say, I'm glad I'm not the one who dropped the cake. It seems like I'm always the one doing stuff like that. So please make a note, it wasn't me this time!"

Shay's dad was examining the bottom of his feet.

"I slipped on something. My foot just slid out from under me."

Then we saw it. So did Mr. L. He bent over, wiped something off his shoe, then he looked at the floor where he slipped. Our eyes followed his gaze and we spotted what he was looking at. He grabbed a paper towel and wiped something off the floor. He held the towel close to his face to examine it.

"It's shortening. How did shortening get on the floor?"

We missed a spot in our clean up. We had a paw in this disaster after all! I looked up at PJ to see his reaction.

"OK, Winthrop, but it wasn't just me, this time. We were both cleaning, so we both are to blame!"

But aside from whoever's fault it was, Shay wasn't going to have a birthday cake! And nobody would ever taste our cake. The best cake ever! It could have been worse, though. Mr. L could have been hurt. I'm so relieved that he wasn't!

"Let me call the bakery right away." Shay's mom seemed to have the situation under control already. "They may have a cake already baked that they can decorate for us. If they can't, we can always get an ice cream cake from the supermarket. You know the kids love ice cream cake."

Just for the record, bears love ice cream cake, too.

"I'll go pick it up. Let me get this cleaned up while you call the bakery. Then let me know where I'm going and what I'm picking up."

"Don't worry about that. I'll clean it up while you're gone." Mrs. L paused and looked around. "How *did* shortening get there?" She looked puzzled.

She went into her office off the kitchen to call the bakery and Shay's dad went upstairs to change his clothes and get the car keys.

"Peej, the least we can do is clean this up."

The wooden butchers block in the middle of the kitchen blocked us from view, but we could hear Mrs. L on the phone with the bakery.

"Grab the trash can." I grabbed the spatula, and as soon as PJ brought the trash can over, I started shoveling the cake into it. We both used paper towels to clean up the floor. It was really messy! Then we got our sponge skates on and cleaned the floor.

"Deja vu, Win!" Remind me later to look

that up, because just between you and me, I have no idea what that means.

We finished cleaning the floor and put the garbage can back just as Shay's mom came into the kitchen. She came over to where the cake had fallen.

"Geez, how did Marty get that cleaned up already? How did I not even notice him in here?" She shook her head.

I looked at PJ and he winked at me with a big grin as we stood at the dining room door peeking in. We heard Mr. L's footsteps as he came back downstairs.

"Shay is just finishing in the tub. Did you call the bakery?"

"Yes, they have a cake! They're decorating it now. They said it would be ready in twenty minutes. I'm so relieved! It's the Bakery House on the corner."

"Yup. I'm on my way." Shay's dad walked out the back door and headed toward the car in the driveway.

Shay's mom opened the door and popped her head out. "Thanks for cleaning up the cake, Marty!"

There was a short pause, then he answered, "What are you talking about?" PJ and I giggled together at that. I think that our relief of knowing another cake was on its way made us giddy. Shay would still have a terrific birthday!

"PJ, we better get upstairs before Shay gets out of the bath!"

PJ and I scrammed upstairs and made it back onto the bed just before Shay came back into the room. When I say we scrammed, you know that it's not as fast as it sounds. By now, you know the drill of PJ and me pushing and pulling each other up each step. But we made it!

We spent the rest of the afternoon upstairs. We heard Mr. L return with the cake, just before Shay's friends started to arrive. We sat on the windowsill in the room across the hall from Shay's room. That room is used as Mr. L's study. He has a desk and files, a couch and a television. He never watches television in there, though. But he does work in his study many evenings. He's an accountant, and there's a time of the year that he calls 'tax season' when he's in there every night. As I understand it, people have to pay taxes. I'm not sure what those are, since that's something bears don't do. But I don't think I'd like it.

PJ wants to be an accountant, so he often goes in there and looks at the stuff Mr. L has done, trying to figure it all out.

He's good with numbers and can count really high without using his claws. Also, he thinks he'd look good wearing those half glasses that all accountants wear. I think it's required or something.

Anyway, we knew Shay's dad would be at the party on the patio all day, and that we'd be safe in there. We had the perfect view of the entire patio and back yard, sitting there on the windowsill in the study. We had a glorious day watching our boy have a terrific birthday.

After a few hours of games, Shay's aunt and uncle arrived. Aunt Samantha carried in lots more food for the party and helped Shay's mom. Shay's dad and Uncle Benjamin disappeared for a little while.

At that point, we had no idea where they went. Then we heard a lot of noise in the living room. So PJ and I crept down the steps to check out what they were up to. Yes, we bears are a curious lot.

We couldn't take the cubway this time; there was too great a chance of getting caught. So we quietly jumped down each step. We hid behind the newel post on the landing halfway down the stairs, where we hid from Shay's mom yesterday. From there, we could peek around and see what was going on in the living room.

Shay's dad and uncle were setting up a yellow bike for Shay with a big red bow on it!

Oh my gosh, he'd be so excited. It was the exact bike that was on the posters in his room.

There were a few wrapped presents sitting beside the bike.

Then, Uncle Benji (that's what Shay calls him) picked up a bag and reached in—and you'll never guess what he pulled out. A white teddy bear! He was about PJ's size and was wearing a blue sweater with a snowflake on it. How appropriate! A polar bear with a snowflake sweater! But wait—if a polar bear likes the cold, why would he need a sweater? Hmmm. Anyway, he was a handsome bear.

Uncle Benji put the bear on the seat of the bicycle and said to him, "You sit here, little fellow. You'll make a great surprise." Then he and Shay's dad left the room, went outside, and joined the party. I *knew* Uncle

Benji was a bear lover!

It was quiet in the house now, but you could hear all the commotion and laughter and joy outside.

We were still behind the post on the stairs peeking into the living room. We saw the little white bear looking around. He saw us and got a scared look on his face. Of course! He didn't know us at all. So PJ and I both waved to him and smiled to let him know he had friends here.

He gave us a huge smile and waved back. Now I couldn't wait to meet him!

Chapter Six
Another Mystery

It was a long day for PJ and me. After all, we had been up all night baking that cake. Don't get me wrong. It was a great day. We loved seeing Shay having a terrific birthday. But we were really tired.

After a day full of playing in the backyard with all his friends, the cookout—with more food than you can imagine—was pure torture for PJ and me. We were sitting in the window, watching everybody eat and smelling all the wonderful food. You know how much we love to eat! Well, we got to raid the leftovers later.

After the cookout, there was birthday cake, which should have been the one that PJ and I made. Well, really it should have been the first cake Mrs. L bought, but you remember what happened to that one. Anyway, there was also ice cream and cookies and fruit and popsicles and, well, so much other amazing stuff we just couldn't wait to get our paws on!

Everybody sang to Shay, then he tried to blow out the candles. But they wouldn't go out. They kept relighting! It was so funny! Shay was laughing. We were laughing really hard, too. Fortunately, the window was closed, so no one could hear us. It was such a great time.

Shay's friends all gave him some really great cards they made. I think he'll cherish them forever. Whenever somebody makes you something, it's really special. It seems they have actually given a part of themselves to you when they make something for you. The moms all handed Mrs. L envelopes when they dropped off their kids for the party. I guess those were the envelopes for Shay's charity donation.

We loved the party, for sure! But when we discovered the new bear, we were dying to get into the living room to meet him. But Shay's aunt and uncle were hanging out in the living room area. They were really here for a family celebration after the kids' party. But with them around, we couldn't meet the new bear. PJ and I were both really excited to do that. It seemed that we'd have to wait to do that until after the family party when Shay got his bike and he brought him upstairs.

I was in a hurry to put the little bear's fears to rest. I mean, I can only imagine how nervous he was, coming to this new home where he didn't know anybody. He had no idea what to expect for his new life here. I wanted to let him know that he's now in a great home with great people.

Eventually it started to get dark outside. You could tell that PJ was tired. His eyelids were starting to droop and he kept yawning. But he was fighting the sleepiness.

"Win, I sure could use a cup of espresso."

> Shay had to do a report on the world's most popular drink: Coffee. So I learned all about it. Espresso is a concentrated coffee drink that originated in Turin, Italy in 1884 when Angelo Moriondo filed a patent for the first espresso machine.
>
>
>
> Caffeine, a stimulant substance found in coffee and many other plants, acts as a pesticide, keeping insects from destroying the plant. This caffeine stuff gives PJ tons more energy than normal, and makes him stay awake all night. I stay away from the stuff.

"First of all, Peej, how are you going to get that? And second, if you did have some, you'd be bouncing off the walls and swinging from the lights like a monkey! Remember the one and only time you had espresso?"

"Yeah, I was so revved up! I could use that pick-me-up, right about now."

I was tired too. We couldn't wait for the kids to go home so Shay could get his bike.

Finally the party started to wind down and the kids' parents came and picked them up. Shay and his parents said their goodbyes to the guests in the driveway, then returned to the patio and the big mess left from the party. They spent a few minutes outside, then came into the house. They each carried in a platter of food and set them down on the kitchen table and butcher block.

"Why don't we save the cleanup for later?" Shay's mom said. "Let's all go into the living room and visit. The boys haven't seen Benji and Sam for a few weeks. I can clean this up later."

It was just Mr. and Mrs. L, Uncle Benji and Aunt Samantha and Shay's best friend, Thiago, from next door. Sometimes Thiago is called Tiggy, or just Tig for short. Oh, and Shay was there, too, of course.

PJ and I were hiding on the landing behind the post again. As you can tell, we like that spot. We had a perfect view.

You should have seen Shay's face light up as he came into the living room and saw the bike. Oh my gosh, it was so great. He was wishing for that bike, but when he didn't get it at the party with his friends, he probably thought he wasn't going to get it. So to actually see that he got it was so exciting for him. I was all giddy again.

Uncle Benji and Aunt Samantha gave him season tickets to the Bulldogs, his favorite baseball team. That was a big hit! They said they would take Shay and Tig to every home game and buy them hot dogs, popcorn, and pretzels at the games. I wish I could go. And of course, the little white bear was a big hit, too. Shay loved him!

Tig gave Shay a left-handed baseball mitt. Did I mention that Shay is a south paw?

It seemed they were all comfortably settled in the living room and were going to be chatting awhile. Everyone seemed tired, and not likely to leave the comfortable seats anytime soon. After all, they were hustling all day with the party, running around with the games, serving food, and having a great time.

Shay and Tig were examining his new bike and everybody seemed to be talking at the same time. PJ and I decided to head into the kitchen to check out the platters of food. We were mighty hungry, as well as tired.

With our superior sense of sniff, we could tell what was on the platters even before we climbed up on the counter. I smelled char-grilled burgers and hot dogs, but that smell was overpowered by barbecued chicken and ribs. I LOVE barbecue! It's sweet and tangy and oh-so good.

So I headed first to the barbecued chicken and ribs. Oh my gosh, was it good. Next to the chicken was a bowl of coleslaw. Mrs. L makes great coleslaw. She puts honey in it, which you know I love. But cabbage gives me the wind, so I decided not to have any of that. Besides, I wanted to save room for birthday cake.

"Win, I feel like such a carnival! I'm just loving all this meat! Chicken, burgers, ribs, hot dogs . . . yum!

THE MEMOIRS OF WINTHROP LITTLE

I started to laugh. "Peej, you mean *carnivore*."

"Oh, whatever I mean, I'm loving it all!"

I, on the other paw wanted to try a bunch of stuff. There was a platter across the room on the butcher block next to the cake, with fresh fruit cut up on long sticks. There was a bowl of vanilla yogurt with honey and orange zest for dipping the fruit. Oh my gosh, that's so yummy gabummy! Well, it has honey in it, need I say more? That stuff is better than candy!

PJ and I had a heyday stuffing our faces with chicken, ribs, burgers, fruit, and yogurt— and of course, birthday cake.

I thought about suggesting to PJ that we clean up the kitchen while everybody was in the living room. But having done that last night, and then cleaning up the cake Mr. L dropped this morning, the thought of cleaning up again was overwhelming. I guess I was just way too tired. And the Littles would really have been confused to find a clean kitchen. So it's better that we didn't.

I had no idea how long we were in the kitchen feasting when we finally heard our people starting to move about in the living room. It seemed like the adults finally wanted to have some time to themselves.

"Shay, why don't you and Tig go upstairs and play while your father, aunt and uncle, and I clean up the party?" Shay's mom was giving the boys a chance to leave and have some time on their own. "In fact, why don't you boys put on your pajamas, so when you get tired, you can just crawl into bed."

Tig was staying the night. Tig and Shay often stay at each other's houses for sleepovers. We don't particularly like that though. When Shay is at Tig's house, we don't get to cuddle with him. And when Tig is here, we sleep on the chair in the corner of the bedroom. The chair is comfortable enough. It's just that we like to be with Shay. If you were a bear, you'd understand. Sometimes after the boys fall asleep, though, we sneak over to the bed. We have to return to the chair before either of them wakes up. We've had some close calls!

The living room party was breaking up.

"Oh my gosh, Peej, we have to get upstairs, fast!"

We had a little time, though. The boys didn't come up immediately. They said good night to Uncle Benji and Aunt Sam, so we were on the bed by the time we heard them coming up the stairs.

"Winthrop!" PJ sounded panicked.

THE MEMOIRS OF WINTHROP LITTLE

"You've got barbecue sauce all over your face!"

Oh my gosh, what was I going to do? I couldn't be seen like that!

The only thing I could do—I pulled the bedspread down and wiped my face on the pillowcase. PJ helped out by licking my face, but could only get a few licks in when Shay and Tig came into the room. I think we got most of it off though. We'll have to take care of that pillowcase tomorrow, if we get a chance. I hope I don't forget!

Shay brought the little white bear up with him and put him on the bed right next to PJ and me. We couldn't talk to him since the boys were right there. We found out later his name is Tyler. I don't think that he's as mischievous as PJ and I are, but I don't think he's a snitch, either. He doesn't seem like the KGB type.

Since we couldn't talk to Tyler, I turned my head ever so slightly and moved my eyes just enough to see him. He was looking at me. I smiled at him so he'd know that we were glad to have him here.

WINTHROP LITTLE

Geez, I hope I didn't have any food in my teeth! He'd think I'm a real slob.

I hate that.

Shay and Tiggy were lying on their bellies, rehashing the events of the day. It sounded like they had a great time. Shay loved his bike and baseball mitt, and was so glad all his friends could share his special day. They looked at the cards that all his friends made. They were all pretty nice, but, well, I could

THE MEMOIRS OF WINTHROP LITTLE

have done better. But Shay loved them, and that's what counts.

After the boys had been chatting awhile, we heard Shay's dad and uncle coming upstairs. They were headed to the study.

"I'm interested to hear what you think of the plans," Mr. Little was saying, "Some minor renovations will make a big difference to this house. Marie would love to get the laundry out of the basement and up to the second floor. And I'd love to make Shay's room a little larger."

Marie is Shay's mom's name.

They went into the study and were there for quite some time, looking at the plans, I guess, before they came into Shay's room to chat with the boys. They were talking about the opening game coming up soon.

"Guys," Shay's mom burst into the room, "I went down to the basement to put the table cloths into the laundry and I found a half-eaten cake behind the washing machine. Do any of you know anything about that? Where did that cake come from?"

Everybody looked so confused. I nudged PJ to keep him from laughing out loud. I was worried that somehow Shay would get blamed.

"It's so odd," she went on. "From what I

could tell, it looked like the birthday cake, but dad dropped that cake on the kitchen floor and put it in the garbage can. I guess we have another mystery in this house that we'll never be able to solve."

Everybody just looked dumbfound. There was silence. Of course nobody suspected us . . . right? At that moment, Willie-B looked directly at us . . . like he knew something.

Do you have any little mysteries like this in your house?

Are your bears as innocent as they look!?

ABOUT THE AUTHOR

Winthrop Little has written the first book in a series of his memoirs, chronicling growing up in a suburban American family. He writes in the first-bear, stream of consciousness literary style. This is the first glimpse into the clandestine lives of teddy bears. Like Alexander Solzhenitsyn, Winthrop Little breaks the silence.

Made in United States
Orlando, FL
24 January 2023

29029472R00049